Hugs from the Thrift Store Bears
and Olive Evans

With love & hugs from
all the Thrift Store Bears

Many thanks to my friends, family and The Wellness Community family
for their encouragement and support;
to Jim Furmston, whose music brings the bears to life;
to Jonathan Evans, Alex Harris and Terry Mercer for technical help,
and especially to my husband David, for his loving care.
Olive

Dedicated to Teddy Bear lovers everywhere and
to my husband Jack, who helped me conceive the idea of Teddy Traveler
over twenty years ago as we walked up a hill in Idyllwild,
California. From this idea came Bearly Impressions and
numerous Teddy Bear paintings.
Pat

Music dedicated to my wife Karen.
Jim

Library of Congress Cataloging-in-Publication Data

Evans, Olive 1933-

The Thrift Store Bears / poems by Olive Evans ; illustrations by Patricia Woolley - 1st ed.

Summary: Twenty-seven original poems for children

ISBN # 0-9748954-0-7

1. Children's poetry, American (1. American poetry) 2. Teddy Bears-Poetry 3. American Poetry

1. Evans, Olive

Teddy Traveler books are available at special discounts for bulk purchases, for sales promotions,

premiums, fund-raising, or educational use. Special editions or book excerpts can also be created

to specification.

For details contact - Teddy Traveler, P.O. Box 3223, 15th St. Manhattan Beach CA 90266.

Website: teddytraveler.com

Library of Congress Control Number: 2004093277

Printed in Taiwan

Contents

THE THRIFT STORE BEARS' SONG

We're the Thrift Store Bears, yes, the Thrift Store Bears.
We live happily together in a sunny room downstairs,
In an old two-storied redwood house, not far from the sea,
The coziest home for teddy bears, on that we all agree.

We're the Thrift Store Bears, yes, the Thrift Store Bears.
Brand new bears are welcome, but they mustn't put on airs.
We shelter dogs and dragons if they promise not to bite.
We don't have many house rules, but we're not allowed to fight.

We're the Thrift Store Bears, yes, the Thrift Store Bears.
We are different shapes and sizes, but each one of us shares
Our stories, our adventures, our laughter and our lunch.
Friends and neighbors call us a very merry bunch
Of Thrift Store, Thrift Store
Thrift Store Bears.

TINY BEAR

I never ever wanted to be a tiny bear.
Large bears always passed me with their noses in the air.
And I was often stamped on, stepped on, sat on and squooshed,
Trampled on, leaned on, pulled around and pushed.

Now one day I decided I'd really had enough.
A bear like me who's thin and small, must learn to ACT TOUGH.
I came to the conclusion that exercise would be
An excellent way to strengthen my frail anatomy.
So I jumped and skipped, I hopped and flipped,
I ran around ten blocks.
I did one hundred sit-ups. I lifted heavy rocks.

So now when large bears push me or try to knock me down,
I push them back and show them I'm the strongest bear in town.

And from that day to this I have never ever been
Stamped on, stepped on, sat on or squooshed,
Trampled on, leaned on, pulled around or pushed.

Y I P P E E !

BIGLEY BEAR'S STORY

Before I was found in a Thrift Store
Back when I was three,
I lived in a house with a hundred rooms,
And at four we had afternoon tea.

Now afternoon tea sounds special,
And the food was certainly nice.
Sandwiches, cakes and biscuits,
No lumpy porridge or rice.
Then one day I dropped my sandwich.
It fell in my cup of tea.
The tea splashed all over the table,
And some of it splattered on me.

I jumped up, and horror of horrors!
My tea cup sailed through the air,
And broke into hundreds of pieces
As it hit a large antique chair.
My master rang for the butler,
And the butler took me upstairs
To a dusty room called "the attic,"
Where I met some dusty bears.

The bears had been there for ages.
"We don't like it here," they said.
"Then let's run away," I whispered,
"When everyone's gone to bed."
At midnight we crawled through a window
And on to the roof of the house.
Then we slid down a rusty old drainpipe,
And almost fell on a mouse.

"It's raining bears!" she squeaked loudly.
"I cannot believe my eyes.
I've heard of it raining cats and dogs.
Could you be dogs in disguise?"
We said, "We are bears, and we're friendly."
She said, "Are you running away?"
We said, "Yes," so she offered to show us
A place where we could stay.

So that's how we came to the Thrift Store,
With the help of that brave little mouse.
And one day a lady bought us
And took us all to her house.
I love it here, it's so friendly.
It's a home where everyone cares.
And afternoon teas are a thing of the past -
We have picnics - they're perfect for bears.

BUBBLES AND SQUEAK, THE HIDE-AWAY BEARS

Where is Bubbles? Where is Squeak?
They're not in the garden or down by the creek.
It's almost their bedtime. Where can they be?
Are they hiding in the closet or climbing up a tree?

"I think," said Daisy Bear in a very loud voice,
"I'll have to give these bedtime treats to Jimmy Bear and Joyce.
Tonight it's honey cookies and pink lemonade.
Those bears aren't here to eat them, I'm very much afraid."

"I'm here," shouted Bubbles. "I'm here," shouted Squeak.
"We've finished our game of hide-and-go-seek.
We'll both take a bath, and we'll soon be super clean.
We'll be the cleanest teddy bears the world has ever seen.
We'll shampoo our fur and we'll scrub our dirty feet.
Then when it's time to go to bed,
Could we please, please, please have that bedtime treat?"

BABY BEAR

I'm an ordinary kind of bear
That no-one looks at twice.
My ears and arms and legs are small,
Nobody says "You're nice."
One eye is bigger than the other
And both are black and tiny.
My nose is on the shapeless side -
It isn't round or shiny.
My name is quite forgettable,
I'm known as "Baby Bear."
I'm not sure where I came from -
No-one seems to care.
But guess what? I'm a happy bear,
I'm never, ever glum,
Because I came into the world
With a rattle in my tum!
And when I jump up in the air
Or shake myself around,
That rattle comes alive and makes
A chirpy, chuckly sound.

When I look into a mirror
I can see I'm ordinary.
But inside of me, where my rattle lives,
I'm EXTRAORDINARY!

MILLICENT CLAIRE, THE CHATTERBOX BEAR

I'm Millicent Claire, the chatterbox bear,
I chatter day and night.
Chatter, natter, chitter-chat,
I'm a chatterbox delight!
Now, can you keep a secret? I promised not to tell,
But Roland bear said yesterday he wasn't feeling well.
He ate some beetroot-raisin sauce that Charlie Chef had made.
His stomach's feeling queasy, so he's resting in the shade.
And Primrose bear told me today that someone large had sat
Upon the wooden kitchen chair that holds her Sunday hat.
The hat was round and very tall, but now it's very flat.
And did you know that Baxter and his brothers, Bob and Bill
Found a very dirty rubber tire and rolled it down the hill?
The tire ran away from them - they couldn't make it stop.
It headed for the window of Mr. Jenkins' shop.
It hit the glass, and now the bears must work for Mr. J.
Because the window's smashed to bits, and guess who has to pay?
(Baxter, Bob and Billy Bear can't play outside today).
There's so much more to tell you, but it's getting very late.
It's time for me to go to bed; the news will have to wait.
I'll get up in the morning when the birds begin to cheep.
I'll find out what is going on while you're still fast asleep.
Then I'll chatter in the morning,
I'll natter late at night.
I'm Millicent Claire, the chatterbox bear,
I'm a chatterbox delight!

HUNNY BEAR'S COMPLAINT

I'm an overstuffed bear who loves honey:
A natural state of affairs,
For everyone knows where there's honey
There's always bound to be bears.

You might think my life is quite perfect,
I'm a bear who is easy to please.
But often, while eating my honey,
I'm pestered by large bumble bees.

I've asked them to be less aggressive,
And I've offered them honey for free.
But that doesn't make any difference -
They prefer the honey on me!

MIKE THE MOTORCYCLE BEAR

I'm a wild and woolly bear known as Motorcycle Mike.
I wear goggles and a helmet, but I haven't got a bike.
So I conjure up a motorbike in my imagination,
The kind of bike that I can ride to any destination.
And when I want to go somewhere I jump up on the bed
And shout aloud to all my friends: "Find a helmet for your head,
And you can come along with me on a super, fun-filled ride.
My magic bike can hold us all." Their smiles grow one mile wide.
When everyone has settled down, I shout: "Now hold on tight."
And we zoom boom through the doorway like a rocket-blasting kite.
V-R-O-O-M!
The bears are always thankful when we reach home safe and sound.
They say they love to fly up high, but it's safer on the ground.
We talk about the fun we've had and the places we have been,
And we sit and plan more mystery rides - there's lots we haven't seen.
Oh, how I love my motorbike, on the ground or in the air.
With a VROOM, VROOM, VROOM, and a ZOOM, ZOOM, ZOOM,
I'm the motorcycle bear.

FRED THE FIX-IT BEAR

The fix-it bear, that's me
You don't have to pay me: I'm free.
I can fix flat tires and oil dirty locks.
I can dig up your garden and throw out all the rocks.
I can stop faucets dripping, I repair broken clocks.
The only things I can't fix are the holes in my socks.

(But I'm learning)

SCRAPPY THE ARKANSAS BEAR

I'm Scrappy, the Arkansas Bear.
I'm carefree and totally charming.
I'm made out of curtains and worn-out p.j.s,
Odd scraps of cloth that have seen better days.

There are stitches all over my body.
Someone spent hours making me.
My arms and my legs are quite floppy and fat.
My edges are frayed - I don't care about that.

I'm the very first recycled bear.
I'm old now, and some seams are splitting.
But I'm tough and I'm rough, I'm flappy and zappy,
And not only that, I'm amazingly happy
Because I'm the Arkansas Bear, yeah!
Because I'm the Arkansas Bear.

MARY LOUISE AND HER PESKY DISEASE

Mary Louise has a pesky disease,
It's not in the dictionary.
No sign of a wheeze, a sniffle or sneeze,
And it's certainly not beriberi.

This unfortunate bear has more than her share
Of misfortunes quite rare and unique.
She fell off a chair while eating a pear,
And couldn't sit down for a week.

When she fell from a tree we took her to see
A clever old Doctor called Titus.
He said: "Deary me, it's easy to see
You are suffering from Accidentitus."

"It WILL go away as long as you stay
As still and as quiet as a stone.
Forget about play, stay in bed every day.
I'll check on your progress by phone."

"I'll keep the disease," said Mary Louise.
"Bumps, scratches and knocks aren't so bad.
I'll sing with the bees and climb in the trees.
If I sit like a rock, I'll go mad!"

So Mary Louise often falls out of trees,
But wherever she goes you'll hear laughter.
She may scrape both her knees and be chased by the bees,
But happily, she'll live ever after.

GRANDPA BEAR

Grandpa Bear says laughter is like a sunny day.
It lifts up soggy spirits, and chases clouds away.
When he tells his funny stories, the bears can't stand up straight.
They roll around with laughter, and even when it's late
They shout: "Don't stop now, Grandpa. Tell one more story, please."
And the smallest bears jump up and down and clamber on his knees.
They like to hear about the time he painted himself green,
When everyone mistook him for a furry lima bean.
We know that Grandpa's life has had its share of ups and downs,
But he believes in laughter, and rarely ever frowns
Or makes a fuss when things go wrong. He tells a tale instead
To cheer himself and all the bears before they go to bed.

DANNY THE VERY SHY BEAR

I'm very, very shy.
Nobody's told me why.
I sometimes want to cry.

I hate to be alone
Like a leaf the wind has blown
And left beneath a stone.

I'm frightened of the dark,
Dogs scare me when they bark.
I wish I were a shark.

I've always been this way.
Excuse me, did you say
You'll play with me today?

You did? Oh, what a treat!
I'm very pleased to meet
Some-one so kind and sweet.

Shall we play at let's pretend?
It's fun to have a friend.
That's how happy stories end.

MAXIE, THE YODELING BEAR

Sometimes in the springtime when the bears are still in bed
Maxie wakes up early with a yodel in his head.
It doesn't happen often, but the moment that it does
His chest begins to wobble, and his throat begins to buzz.
"Look out," he warns the sleepy bears, "A yodel's on its way.
I don't know how to stop it! Today's a yodeling day."
So he yodel ays and he yodel oos, and he yodel ees as well.
And when he needs to rest his voice, he shakes an old cowbell.
Maxie says that yodelers who stand on mountain tops
Can hear their echoes bounce around - their yodeling never stops.
He doesn't have a mountain, so he stands on the topmost stair,
Joyfully singing his yodeling song to each sleepy thrift store bear.

PINKY'S HATS

Pinky has a scrap bag, and this is what is in it:

Red ribbons, blue bows, buttons and a feather,
Glass beads, white cards, a sprig of lucky heather,
Candy-striped cotton, taffeta and felt,
Gold and silver coins from a pirate's leather belt.
Moonstones, smooth stones found near the shore,
Sea shells, tinkly bells, and much, much, more.
And while the thrift store bears take their afternoon naps,
Pinky sits and sorts through her special bag of scraps.

And this is what she makes:

Lacy hats with ribbons for lizards, snakes and frogs,
Flowery hats for spiders, dizzy hats for dogs.
Beaded hats for hummingbirds, feathered ones for cats.
Frilly hats for friendly mice, but none for mean old rats.
Button hats with bobbles for bears who like to dance,
Hats of silk and satin for trips to Paris, France.

You can search the whole world over, but you'll never, ever find
Hats that look like Pinky's hats - they're one of a kind.

22

AUNT LIL

Aunt Lil is a quiet and tiny bear.
We think she's extremely ancient.
She wears a small hat that's dusty and black.
She's kind and always patient.

Aunt Lil knits colorful woolen squares,
Which she carefully sews together
To make rainbow blankets for each little bear
Who feels cold in the wintry weather.

Aunt Lil is a quiet and tiny bear.
We think she's a perfect treasure.
So we gave her a medal. It said "WE LOVE YOU."
She said not a word, but every bear knew
That her heart was brimming with pleasure.

CHARLIE, CHEF EXTRAORDINAIRE

I'm Charlie, a bear who loves cooking,
And I'm hoping that one day I'll be
The kind of Chef who's world-famous.
"The Amazing Chef Charlie," that's me.

I make the most wonderful sauces.
No-one creates them like me.
Each sauce is a mouth-watering pleasure.
When you've tried one, I know you'll agree.

I adore my sardine sauce special.
Chopped seaweed gives it a crunch.
Combined with raw eggs and minced shell-fish,
It makes a great sea-faring lunch.

But none of my bear friends will try it.
"We're not very hungry," they say.
"We've eaten already." "We're feeling unwell,"
Then everyone hurries away.

Each day I create superb sauces.
I don't know what else I can do.
I wish someone nice would come over
And try them. I wonder - would you?

LITTLE PETE

I used to be a skinny bear
And I had a nervous stutter,
Until the day I came across
A jar of peanut butter.

Now when I saw that peanut butter
Sitting on the shelf,
I immediately decided
To try some for myself.

I carefully opened up the lid
And then dipped in my paw.
The taste was so delicious
I had to have some more.

But Charlie Chef came through the door
And caught me by surprise.
"A PEANUT BUTTER THIEF" he roared,
"Right here before my eyes."

I tried to speak, but oh dear me,
Not one word could I utter
Because my mouth was firmly stuck
With crunchy peanut butter.

"Wom werry worree, Warly Wev,"
Was all that I could say.
Charlie Chef began to laugh,
Then said: "Don't go away."

He poured me out a glass of milk.
I drank it very slowly.
I noticed that my once thin tum
Was looking roly-poly.

"Thank you Charlie Chef," I said.
"I love that peanut butter."
"My goodness," Charlie Chef replied,
"You spoke without a stutter!"

I don't know how it came about,
But ever since that day
I don't look skinny any more,
And my stutter's gone away!

HENRIETTA, THE HUMMING BEAR

Henrietta Bear has a talent that is rare,
Everybody loves to hear her humming.
Every minute of the day is always spent that way,
Henrietta Bear likes to hum.
Bumblebees and hummingbirds ask daily for advice.
This week she's giving lessons to a family of mice.
They come to see her twice a week.
They say she's very nice.
Henrietta's famous for her humming.

HAPPY H. HUGGINS

Are you feeling unwanted and misunderstood?
Are you feeling deep down in the dumps?
Are there clouds in the sky that won't go away?
Does your oatmeal have too many lumps?

Then it's time to see Happy H. Huggins.
Happy H. Huggins, that's me.
I'll soon cheer you up with a custom-made hug,
For hugs are my specialty.

I can give you a hug that is dreamy, or wild,
Or you might like a combination.
A kiss and a hug, or a pat and a hug?
Each one is a Huggins creation.

So the moment a black cloud descends on your head
Come over, my bear hugs are free.
And if ever I'm feeling in need of a hug,
Could you possibly give one to me?

29

THE GRUMP

I'm a first-class grump on Monday,
And by Friday I'm so mean,
I growl and scowl, I stamp and howl,
I'm sure no-one has seen
A bear in such a nasty mood, a bear who likes to be
A snarly, gnarly, stingy, wingey, MIS-ER-Y.

On Saturdays and Sundays
I sometimes crack a smile.
It doesn't last for very long -
Smiling's not my style.
I like to sneer, I often jeer, I think it's cool to be
A snarly, gnarly, stingy, wingey, MIS-ER-Y.

Holidays are horrendous,
I hate St. Valentine's Day.
The Easter Bunny's scared of me,
He always hops away.
And no-one sends a Christmas card to a bear who loves to be
A snarly, gnarly, stingy, wingey, MIS-ER-Y.

GRRRRRRRRRR!

AMANDA THE DANCING BEAR

Amanda bear dances
Like a flame in the fire:
With a sizzle, a twizzle, a fiery fizzle.
Like a teasing breeze:
With a twirl, a whirl, a sudden swirl.
Like a hide-and-seek leaf:
With a wobble, a wiggle, a jelly bean jiggle.
Like a sunbeam,
a moonbeam,
a glittering star beam.
From morning to night
Amanda bear dances.

THE RAINBOW BEAR

Pink and purple, blue and green
Are the colors of the Rainbow Bear.
Soft and smooth as velveteen,
She dreams in the wicker chair
Of a shimmering bow in a rain-drenched sky
Where she always played in days gone by.
Slipping and sliding down a rainbow path,
Popping colored bubbles in a rainbow bath.

Pink and purple, blue and green
Are the colors of the Rainbow Bear.
Soft and smooth as velveteen,
She wakes in the wicker chair
And remembers that her rainbow disappeared one day,
Leaving only memories that never fade away.
So she sings rainbow lullabies when nights are long,
Turning darkness into light with her rainbow song.

TED THE BAG BEAR

Someone left a bag on our doorstep last night.
It wasn't there on Friday afternoon.
It's a small canvas bag, but something's not quite right.
It's moving and it's singing a tune.

It's hopping up the steps. It's knocking at the door,
And a voice is saying: "Anyone at home?"
It sounds quite nice and friendly, it doesn't shriek or roar.
Could it be a homeless garden gnome?

"It's probably a bear in a bag," Henry said.
(Henry Bear is almost always right).
So we peeped out the door and a bear said "Hi, I'm Ted.
Could my bag and I stay here for tonight?"

We told Ted and his bag they could come and live with us,
So they moved into our house by the sea.
And whenever bears play in his bag, he never makes a fuss.
He says he likes to have their company.

GRANNY WINKLE

When Granny Winkle comes to stay
We climb up on her lap
And stroke the soft fur on her ears,
Then she takes a tiny nap.
We love our Granny very much,
She means the world to us.
She tells us we're her special bears,
And she never makes a fuss
If we spill our milk on the polished floor
Or splash in a muddy puddle.
Granny Winkle cleans us up
Then gives us all a cuddle.

JACK THE BRAVE

If there's something strange and scary in your closet,
If a slimy snake is slithering near your toes,
If a monster from a deep lagoon with seaweed in his hair
Wants to blacken both your eyes and twist your nose,
DON'T WORRY, there's a bear called Jack who'll help you,
And so will his assistant, Freddy Mouse.
They'll be over in a flash with a special box of tools,
And they'll check out every monster in your house.

Freddy Mouse takes care of Jack's red toolbox,
Which holds a can of bubbles and a rope,
A flashlight and a whistle, a tube of stick-fast glue,
A jar of cheese and honey, and some soap.
Glue quickly stops a slimy snake from slithering
And skeletons in the closet hate the glow
Of Jack's fluorescent flashlight when he shines it on their bones.
"It's Jack the Brave," they shriek, and off they go.

Old monsters aren't so easy to dispose of.
Sometimes Jack can tie them up with rope.
But often two or three will chase him up a tree,
And that's when Jack says: "Freddy, get the soap."
When broken up and scattered on the side-walk,
The soap looks just like chunks of cheddar cheese.
The monsters eat the scented soap, then quickly feel unwell
And disappear like ghosts behind the trees.

It's time to party when the danger's over.
So Freddy whistles a happy marching tune.
Jack Bear eats his honey, and Freddy eats his cheese,
Then everyone blows bubbles at the moon.

THE THRIFT STORE SING-ALONG BAND

Billy Bear and Ben sing "diddley-dum"
In the Thrift Store Sing-Along Band.
Ruby sings "ting" and Scrappy sings "dong,"
Mary-Lou and Henrietta follow along
With a beep and a boop and a scooby, dooby, doo.
We're the Thrift Store Sing-Along Band.

Bella Bear and Brighton sing "la, la, la,"
In the Thrift Store Sing-Along Band.
Max sings "oomp" and Pete sings "pah."
Gilly Bear and Homer sing "rah, rah, rah."
With a tootle and a toot and a bim, bam, bong,
We're the Thrift Store Sing-Along Band.

Everyone does what Grandpa says
In the Thrift Store Sing-Along Band.
He waves his arms, shouts "One, two, three.
If you want to start together, you'd better watch me!"
We're a super-dooper sing-along, a diddly-dooper ding-along
The greatest Sing-Along Band.

Olive Evans has worked extensively with young children as a teacher, writer, storyteller and director of storytime theater. She was born in England and graduated from Goldsmiths College, London and California State University, Dominguez Hills. She has lived in Manhattan Beach, California since 1968. While going through treatment for cancer, Olive set herself a goal to write a poem about each Teddy Bear she had rescued from thrift stores over the years. This book represents about half of the Bears she rescued. The challenge of writing these poems helped enormously in her recovery.

Pat Woolley is an artist living in Manahattan Beach California. Born in France, Pat studied at the Academie Julian in Paris and at the Art Center College of Design in Los Angeles. Though an avid lover and painter of Teddy Bears, Pat also paints landscapes, figures and still life. Pat travels to Provence, France each year to paint the village scenes and country landscapes she loves. Her work can be found in private collections in the USA and Europe.

Jim Furmston was born in Victoria, Canada and graduated from the University of Victoria with a degree in music. He took an advanced degree at the University of Southern California and now lives in Los Angeles. Jim is in demand as a performer of classical music, as a jazz pianist and as a musical director. He also composes for TV, film and stage and has taken part in the Los Angeles Philamonic's school outreach program.